I0210794

A Poetry Collection

Soul of a Rising Phoenix

EMMA DESULME

Copyright © 2021 by Emma Desulme
All rights reserved. No part of this publication may be reproduced, distributed, or transmitted in any form or by any means, including photocopying, recording, or other electronic or mechanical methods, without the prior written permission of the publisher, except in the case of brief quotations embodied in critical reviews and certain other non-commercial uses permitted by copyright law. For permission requests, email the publisher, addressed "Attention: Permissions Coordinator," at the email address below.

ISBN: 978-0-578-32712-9 (paperback)

First printing edition 2021.

Written, illustrated, designed, and edited by Emma Desulme

www.soulofarisingphoenix.com
info.soulofarisingphoenix@gmail.com

Dedication

I dedicate this book to:
- My past, present and future self.
- Anyone who's ever felt uncomfortable outside of their comfort zone. You can do it. It's never too late to be great. You have more in you than you realize.

Acknowledgments

I thank God, because without Him I wouldn't be able to do any of this.

"Life begins at the end of your comfort zone."

— Neale Donald Walsch

Preface

I always knew that I was going to write this book, but somewhere along the lines of life, trauma, and dream stealers, I never did.

This poetry book started when I was 12. I had **very** deep feelings and experienced more events than someone should ever have to experience at that age. Writing became my therapy. It was the outlet I needed to express my emotions, struggles, victories, and experiences. Poetry is all about the freedom of expression. Whatever you write, is right. I love how it creates a no judgment zone. The pieces you will read, ranges from preteen into my adulthood.

So why did I finally decide to publish my book now? Well... I discovered the more I dove into personal development, the more I started to believe I could, I should, so I did.

Les Brown, the motivational speaker said it best "The graveyard is the richest place on earth, because it is here that you will find all the hopes and dreams that were never fulfilled, the books that were never written, the songs that were never sung, the inventions that were never shared, the cures that were never discovered, all because someone was too afraid to take that first step, keep with the problem, or determined to carry out their dream." That is something I didn't want I know that I am destined for more in life.

Table of Contents

Table of Contents

Welcome!

Welcome to my thoughts.

I hope you enjoy my book,

With great pleasure and delight.

Thank you in advance for taking your time,

To join me on this journey and

On this interesting ride.

These words are here for all to see.

Sorry Mom and Dad for the use of my profanity.

This book really challenged me, but in a good way.

Let me no longer delay and send you on your way.

"If the size of the vision that you have for your life isn't intimidating to you, there's a good chance it is insulting to God."

—Steven Furtick—

Am I?

Am I good enough?
Or am I just fooling myself?
Those thoughts run through my head.
When I wake up in the morning or lay in my bed.
In between those moments,
I start to dread and gloom.
Here comes the Imposter Syndrome,
Seeping in, full Bloom.
Imposer, imposer!
Is what the dummy in my head shouts.
I'm trying to switch the channel.
I'm trying to drown it out.
I waited too long, to step into my greatness.
I think that I finally figured it out.
The dummy, is a dummy for a reason,
Now is the time, and this is my season.

Trapped

It's like a prison in here,

Without any air.

No way to be free,

So, I got on my knee.

I prayed that the war would be over,

So, my family and I could start all over.

I saw a torpedo and I ducked for cover,

Little did I know, it took the life of my little brother.

I went crazy without any care,

But like they say,

God doesn't give us anything we can't bare.

Open

To be open, means to be weak; vulnerable.

Just open for the hurt to destroy you.

To be open, means you're accepting the fact that your

Heart can be torn into shreds.

Stepped on with combat boots and

Dragged all over the world by slow Hooptie.

Once you're open, you're fucked!

Emotionally, it takes all your life to heal and to deal.

And maybe you're so hurt from your "Chance"

That you'll never open up to anyone else.

Even if you and that person is meant to be.

You'll be too hurt to see.

Lost

I'm lost in a sea of sinful bliss
Allowing anyone to give me a kiss,
Open to the new ideas of impure thoughts
Inhaling the toxins that corrupts my heart
My mind, body and soul are solely yours,
But not completely.
I need your guidance,
So the devil won't defeat me,
And cheat me out of the promised land,
You promised thee.
To serve and protect is their law,
Which comes with many flaws
That's the name of the game
To make servants into slaves and
Protect only the rich and fame
To play God with people's lives and
Simply apologize without remorse
When a whole village cries, for that person who dies
Failing to realize the reprise of it all
That one day, these so-called God's
Will feel the wrath of the Almighty God ruler of all.

Stress

Stress is a killer
Not a life fulfiller
The strain on your heart
The pain in your head
Anxiety plus pressure over brokenness equals dead
With relief out of sight
You always putting up a good fight
It shows your might with delight
But if you don't slow down,
You're about to see the light.
Relaxation creates a good sensation inside of me
Giving me nothing but peace and harmony
Deep breathes and meditation of nothing is what I do
Relaxing every muscle so it feels like goo
Floating down from the sky
Realizing I can't fly!
Jumping out of my bed, knowing it was a dream
Making me see how hard life can be
And taking a vow that still holds now
Stress will not be my killer
As long as I have the Lord as my pillar.

Anxiety + Pressure=DEAD
 Brokenness

Struggle

The flesh is weak.
I mean, duh!
Weak is the flesh, as we all know.
Thus for, making me weak.
A weak-minded female (temporarily).
Especially my Spirituality.
Falling into pieces,
That I so desperately try to piece together
Giving into the temptation.
Saying "Yeah whateva."
I'm in control, fooling myself.
Tryina play mind games and thinking I'm winning.
You'd have to use night goggles, to look through the
Dark, to see how I'm sinning.

And enjoying every moment of it (at the time).
Living in my sinful bliss and feeling Divine
Without a care in the world, feeling so free.
Letting down my hair,
So he can choke me up and grab me
Later hanging my head down, on two accounts.
Dealing with the guilt and the shame.
Damn! Will I ever amount?

Back and forth I go,
From being godly to a hoe!
Where is the relief?
Too many dudes releasing up in me.
I go round and round,
Being chained up and bound.
Literally and Spirituality.

How do I get back to the place?
Where it's just figuratively?
Speaking...
I'm still seeking.... through the rubble,
Can you truly understand... my struggle?

Anger

You fuck with me, put me down, hurt me
I don't say anything because,
The things I want to say maybe too harsh.

You don't know me.
You don't know how I roll.
You bitch ass mother fucker!
At times I wish you never existed.

Mann... things, I think.
The shit that goes on in my motherfucking head!
Could make me hurt or probably kill that fucker!

The shit that pisses me off,
Is that your dumb ass don't even realize it.
But the only thing that doesn't lead to insanity
Is writing my thoughts,
My motherfucking feelings on a piece of paper. SHIT!

Times I'm so hurt,
I don't write.
I don't say anything.
I just keep it to myself bottled up.

"Writing is my therapy.
The outlet I needed when there was

nowhere else to turn."

-Emma Desulme

Child's Play

Hi, my name is Lizzy, and I'm eight years old.
I just had sex with a 20-year-old.
I thought he was my friend,
until he made me bleed.

I cried for days because it hurted when I pee peed.
I feel funny inside and sad sometimes
He said I'll be alright we just have to do it more
But when we do my body feels sore.

I told my mommy about it, she laughed at me.
And said how I became quite the little B.
I don't understand why she said that,
She made me go live with grandma
When I got pregnant.

My friend he lives in a box now,
With monkey bars.
He is not allowed to play with little children
anymore.

24

Hi, my name is Ashely and I'm 13.
You just heard from my mommy and I'm not
gonna let the same happen to me.

Oh yeah that's my daughter smart as can be,

I'm 21 now living with HIV.

When will it End?

(Him, who used his daughter Sophie to summon Lizzy)

Him: *"Come here my daughter and call your little friend for me."*
Sophie: *"Okay, Daddy. Lizzy, Lizzy! My daddy wants you."*
Lizzy: Whispers *"No"* to herself.
Sophie: *"Lizzy!"*

Lizzy: "Fine, I'll go, but let this be known,
The man you call daddy should be thrown in a hole.
Kissing and touching me, whenever we're alone.
Me tryina get away but his hold is just too strong.
Knowing in my heart, what he's doing to me is wrong
When he summons me, I try to prolong,
The hurt and pain he inflicts upon me.
Having flashbacks of the memory that scars me,
Psychologically and mentally
To the point of no escape
Scrubbing my body so hard that it turned red hot,
Like a rage of fire.

Thought about killing him
But turned to a Higher Power.
For strength and redemption, mostly on his part.

26

For him to resist the temptation
Of touching little kid's private parts.
Boys and girls! This is kind of man,
Must be put to a STOP!
I have an idea, let's cut off his cock!
And put it in his mouth.
Give him a taste of his own medicine.
Light his body up with fuel and
Still pray he goes to heaven
I could go on and on, how I could kill that fucker.

As I grew up, I realized he's just a little sucker.
But beware, a lot of them are still out there
Doing the same thing he did to me.
Having you go home silently,
And finding blood in your panties.

Rocking in a corner, saying "Don't grow belly"
The torment and torture is what I endured,
Only wanting to be a kid and nothing more.
Nothing more is what I chant.
NO! STOP THIS! PLEASE NOT FROM THE BACK!!
Tears come out furiously along with blood
He puts a gun in my mouth and asks,
"Who do I love?"
I don't reply, he pulls the trigger...
When will this ever end for Elizabeth "Lizzy" Miller?"

"Poetry is all about the freedom of expression.
Whatever you write is right."

-Emma Desulme

Unspoken

It's easier to write my love, then to say it out loud.

Just letting my pen flow, like I'm on the cloud.

So high from reality, could this be a fantasy?

Imagine me, having the one that makes my heart bleed.

Profusely, continuously I feel you next to me, but can it be?

Or is it in my mind and it's playing tricks on me.

Baby please! I have three words I wanna say to you.

Low and behold, I can't believe these words are true.

But I do... Say what's on my heart?

Or should I pack my bags and part?

Surprise!

Oh shit!

You?

Who knew you and I would become an item?

Why you?

Why me?

Why not he or she?

Is it meant to be?

Don't make me laugh...hehe

I don't like surprises.

They scare me

Next thing you know

I'll be going in a frenzy

Thinking about

Yo, where he be?

Is he cheating on me?

That can't be.

When it's Time

When it's time to love

He lets me know

Even if I want to love before that time

He lets me know

Now, how do I know

He's gonna let me know?

Well, I don't

It's just a feeling that lets me know

That He's letting me know

That it's time to go.

Tied Up

You got me tied up and confused

Not knowing what to do

Frustrated and fucked

Now other people are wishing me good luck

Whipped and beat

Now I face my defeat

So quick with your words

I am no longer flying with the birds

I used to be your Queen and honey

Now you know me as one of your used to B's

The signs were crystal clear

But I was so scared to take a stare

You won, it's over

Now it's my time to start all over

What can I say?

I gave you a try

But deep down inside

You had me tied.

Too Much

I can't write about you, it's too emotional

My flow will become too uncontrollable

What I feel for you is indescribable

The same way you can't explain why I'm so desirable

Emotions running through my veins, Damn!

It's starting to feel like pain

Don't worry my love, I won't go insane

It's just that, with you I'm more sane and complete

Me not having you will be my biggest defeat

The love we have is so pure and raw

If you were to deny my love,

My heart would feel like that guy

Who cut his foot off in Saw

Truth be told, I love it how your mind

Is like a concrete rose

Your love is like a massacre, the only thing I ask of ya

Is a promise that is definite, just like tax and death is

To the soul, your heart is put on death row

Chained and displayed for all to see

Crying like Popeye when he lost his Sweet Pea

Falling like Alicia and playing those wrong keys

I know, I know that's just the way I feel

I'm tryina keep it real,

Factual not fictional

My love for you is as true

As a biblical tale that will never fail.

Dark Side of Bleu's Love

It's crazy how I'm dangerously in love with you.
It's sad but true.
I want you to be my boo,
Don't you know that I love you?
I'll go insane without you.
You complete me, can't you see?
That you and I, we're meant to be.
I cut my wrists enduring oh but so much pain
Not caring if you're the one to blame.
Lying in a puddle of blood,
Knowing you're still in love with Jane.
Mad at the fact that it is I who cannot contain,
Maintain, nor obtain the love that I crave
Which puts me into so much pain.
Sitting here with my knife
Messing with the veins in my brains
Thinking about killing that girl named Jane.
Snap! Back to reality!
Yo! Bleu it's not you!
It's not your fault
He doesn't want to get back with you
So just leave it at that girl, it's not you.

The Dream

My eyes are closed, but I see you so clear.
I stare in your eyes, and the whole world disappears
Leaving us together, so no one can see
Your body moves closer, so you're next to me.
Your fingers unbutton and takeoff my clothes
Your hands moving all over my body,
From my head to my toes.

Without delay, you start to play
Your brown warm fingers will find their own way
It's feeling so good and when I touch you back,
Your long and hard and that makes me wet
I kiss your chest in a rapture sub time
As your fingers playing music in three-quarter time
We're caught in a rapture without a doubt
I push your head lower and you open your mouth

Hours go by; I pick up your face
The look in my eyes, states so simply my case
This pussy is yours and you're gonna take it
If I had said no, you know you would have rapped it
You flipped it, turned it and threw it all around
You found your position, ass up and on the ground
You get behind me and forced it in there,

Pushing whatever is stopping your stroke
You fuck me for hours, like you're going for broke

You've totally flipped out and you're out of control
Your love is insane, and I am your only goal
You're ready to nut, not a minute too soon
I hear my alarm and I'm back in my room
I open my eyes and I hear the door shut
I thought I was dreaming ....
.... but we really did fuck.

True Story

Why must I suffer for loving that guy
That makes me feel good inside.
When he's inside.
Why should I settle for that other guy?
Why am I denied your love, touch, and affection?
When all I need from you,
Is for you to pay a little attention
To my needs, that is my only plea
For this to work, I would need all of thee
Mentally, sexually, deep with intimacy
With little shocks of electricity,
Flowing through my body way past skin deep.

Feeling sensual waves of chills,
Running from the base of my skull down to my feet
Getting palpitations with every rotation
Doing many positions, especially in the kitchen
Spooning til dusk and not giving a fuck
Eating me slow, knowing you know I'll explode!

To a state of relief
Loosening my jaw to stop the grinding of my teeth
The pleasure you bestow upon me is oh so
Memorable, not forgettable
Not to mention real damn pleasurable, enjoyable

Do you feel my heartbeat?
The way you grab me and grind me
To the rhythm of the street and
Make me feel the heat
Your skills are undeniable you're a man of your word
When your face touched my two lips
That's when you really got me turned
Like a feen on trees, kissing me so seductively
You would slide up and down and
Go for rounds and rounds, down to the T
But the fucked-up shit about it, it was only a dream.

I Need You

I need you to... Fuck me, mentally.
Send me into the depths of a deep abyss
With just a sweet tender kiss
Fingering my thoughts
Finger me slow, with your words
I need you to... Fuck me, mentally.
Raw doggy style, but gently.
Master no bating,
Leave me trembling and shaking.
I need you to... Fuck me, mentally.
Lead with your head
As you lead with *your* head
And take me to bed.
I need you to... Fuck me, mentally.
Lick me from my vortex to my cortex,
Got me anticipating that,
 "Good morning beautiful" text, type of sex.
I need you to... Fuck me, mentally.
Give me that brain
As you pick my brain,
While you're spelling my name.
I need you to... Fuck me, mentally.
Pop my pussy, like you popped my cherry,
Got me creaming, no diary.
I. NEED. YOU. TO... Fuck me, mentally.
Flip it, spit on it, then let me sit on it.
Swirl and Twirl,
Enter deep into my world.

Baby, I need you to... Fuck me, mentally.
Savor it, add your flavor to it.
Leave me spellbound as you turn my pages.
I need you to... Fuck me, mentally.
As I exhale,
Study the goosebumps on my body like braille.
I need you to... Fuck me, mentally.
Strategically planting those kisses.
Letting me know that I am your Mrs.
I need you to... Fuck me, mentally.
Hold me. Console me, and never let go of me.

"If you don't know by now,

Let me know, so you can let me go,

So, I can go grow with someone else."

-Emma Desulme

Two

Being girl # 2, a very awkward position.
One, two a.m. doing many sexual positions.
Accepting # 2, puts me in an opposition....
Against myself.
Playing tug-of-war with flesh and love,
Completely kicking my morals out the door.
And I'm okay with that.
Wait....and I'm okay with that!?

We are never far from desperation.
I think I reached my destination.
Unfortunately... Hating the fact you can't be with me,
Won't be with me, shouldn't be with me but you are
(sorta kinda).
I know, I know, this sounds bizarre.
That I wish that we are...

Are we paralyzed by our passion?
Or just blinded by our attraction?
Foolishly allowing a connection
To grow and flow so vibrantly.

Having talks about the future with you and me.
And things from the past we wouldn't want to repeat.
Shhhh.... But we have to be discreet.
Him telling me, "Don't tell nobody we creeping in the
Sheets, or it will be over for us."
Me like a dummy saying, "Don't worry you can trust."

What happened to me?
I went from being a wifey, to stains on your sheets.
No longer high and mighty.
Settled into the fact that
It's ok to be on my knees and not spiritually.

Welcoming the imagery of girl # 2.
You know what they say is true...after hours past two
There are only two things open, legs and drive thru.
Well... You know what?
I'm through, being girl # 2; just a screw.
I deserve better than that. I know that's a fact!

You won't see me laying on my back,
Being a doormat no more.
Because the last time we fucked,
And you walked me to the door
Was the last time you saw me as that whore

New Genre

"I speak Creole and I speak English. Allow me to introduce you to another genre called **Crenglish**!"

-Emma Desulme

Crenglish

Used by Haitian Americans to speak to other Haitians who understand or speak both languages or parts of both languages.

It's actually speaking Creole and English at the same time by alternating from one language to another every 1 or 2 words.

-Urban Dictionary

Inappropriateness

Long time no see,

Damn! You gained weight.

Excuse me Motherfucker!
Do you still want to participate...?
In this life that you have.
Ou pa menm fout konem
Keep talking your shit, I'll turn your ass into grass.
All throughout my life, se kalite moun sa,
I had to deal with.
Poukisa ou pa just fèmen bouch ou
And everything will be alright.

But nooo, that would be too easy,
My Haitians love a fight and
Always think they're right.
You know, the thing that gets me tight,
Is if I really said how I felt about that person,
They would say my parents didn't raise me right.
It's inappropriate for you to mention my weight
This must be one of your stupid character traits.
It's inappropriate for you to ask, "Where's your
man?" And when is **he** going to ask me for *my* hand?
It's inappropriate for you to ask "When are you
having kids?

Respectfully, I need you to mind your biz.
Here's a pop quiz. Tell me real quick.
Does it really matter? Do you even care?
If your answer is "no," then you need to stop and take
a stare...

At your own reflection, cuz you're projecting your
insecurities on me.
Now who's the one whose parents didn't raise them
properly?

Demaskew nan figim,
I need you to get out of my face.
I have no room for your negative energy,
In my space.
That's why I will leave you with this.
Your inappropriateness, that you think it's alright,
Will lead you to say something to the wrong person
and you will surely lose that fight.

I busted out my momma's cochie
Armed and ready…
It's a celebration bitches,
Where's my confetti?

Now… that I've got your attention

Welcome to the Savage Corner!!

Dirty Truth

My style is different,
And is like no other
I'm sorry to let you know,
But I did fuck your brother.
Revenge is so sweet and
Now I hold the meat,
By the balls.
You think you tall?
You ain't shit at all.

My flow is heavy,
Just like my menstrual cycle.
The shit I'm about to tell you,
Will make you go to psycho.
I try to keep things simple
For those who can't understand.
I'll stab you in your nipples,
The day you try to lay your hands, on me.

I'm not crazy nor a Queen B,
But my friends they sometimes call me double D.
Yeah, they're big and round and
Will never go out of style
Juicy and luscious... Uh! You can't touch this!

You think you big?
Well, I'm raw and ruthless
I may have a gap, but boo I ain't toothless

He's been through the wire
I've been through the fire
He blamed it on the rain
I watched her go insane in the brain
Cuz she had so much fame
Can't stop me now boo
I'm too wild to tame!

Not My Business

Yo Rich, be easy!
I know I'm not the one to blame
How was I supposed to know she's psychotic?
And will probably go insane.
Nothings on me, believe you me
Life's too short for me to get all crazy
Yeah, if she wants to fuck, I wish her the best of luck
She ain't tryina to play me
She's only creating a bad image upon thee: self
Me stressing it would only affect my health
Hey shit happens what else can I say
I'm not gonna stop her if she wants to lay...
With him, him, him, or him
I'm not about to make enemies for my friends
Nor defend a person who is denying a helping hand
Life's a hustle, pain is stress
For me? I am not settling for less
It's not my business what you do in cars
Or behind closed doors or
In the alley back of the mall
Just remember that we're living in a war
And whoever you fuck you lose yourself more.

Full

Full my brother? Yes, you are.
FULL OF SHIT!
You whisper nothing but sweet nothings in my ear
Expecting me to fall over with every word that I hear
What are you? Full?
FULL OF SHIT! That's what you are!
Tryina' control thee uncontrollable,
With your lies and your deceits.
Tryina' break the unbreakable,
By destroying their goals and their feats.
You said no once, I asked you twice,
I asked you again, you LIED!
Now I find out that you got a WIFE!

Awww... come on, you know you gonna pay the price
Cuz what we had created a new life.
Surprised my full brother, yes indeedy!
I am no longer the one who is needy.
What we need to do is sign a treaty.
Cuz, you know me, I can get greedy.
Full my brother, my brother who is full.

You are no longer the "MAN" who's full of shit.
You are now known as that SAD, BROKE FUCKER,
 Who's FULL OF SHIT!
And that's about it.

54

Weak Minded Females

Weak minded females...
All around me.
Slipping... into these guys sick perverted fantasies.
Only wanting to abuse you and
Use you to their fullest content.
Watching you open and close like a backyard tent.

Weak minded females, I despise them...
Ya brothers, can't blame them.
They do what they do best.
But I have to admit, ya sometimes go on a quest
Just to get that pussy and drop it like a bad habit
Our females are supposed to be
Slick and quick like a rabbit
But you're not,
You're a weak-minded female who likes it on top,
And always in your mouth.
Kissing his nasty ass feet,
Your biggest mistake,
Wearing your heart on your sleeve.

What's wrong with you? Don't you have any sense?
Please don't tell me you're
Trying to go after his two cents
Be practical, logical, even theoretical
You got these guys,
Eating you up like they the Hannibal.

Darkness falls, upon you weak minded females
Shame and disgust is coated all over your face
You wear many masks trying to cover the disgrace
You don't represent females with
Your beauty and grace
Instead, you let these lawyers cum in you,
Like you're an open and shut case.
Weak minded females open your eyes, not your legs
Stop giving him head
Cuz you'll feel dead inside
Have some pride!

No guy wants a weak-minded chick as a bride
Cuz to them, we're like an envelope
They take what's good inside,
And leave us heart broke
Weak-minded females, this is the last warning
See how pretty that rose is,
But look how sharp that thorn is.

"She is clothed in strength and dignity; and

She laughs without fear of the future."

-Proverbs 31:25.

Letter to My Queens

My oh my, how fly are we...

Strong, beautiful, and gentle as can be.

With our luscious lips and curvy hips.

We. Don't. Take. No. Shit.

Bright and wise,

You'll get lost in our eyes.

With so much flare,

There are men, who are too scared to take a stare.

But that's alright.

Our Kings, who are meant for us

Will stand with us, through that fight.

We are loved, we are mothers.

With skin smooth like butter.

We are united, as sisters,

Filled with so much wisdom.

We are cousins, we are wives.

Who should be honored,

Because we are so divine.

Talented, heroic

You already know it.

Fierce but loving,

Coy and stunning.

With hair of magic

Our hair is one of our crowns.

When it gets done up

It can turn any frown upside down.

Our beauty illuminates,

And yes, people will hate.

Which is why I say this,

To my Queens,

You who radiate,

Always remember,

You are phenomenally great.

"In order to rise from its own ashes,

A Phoenix first must burn."

- Octavia Butler

Her Story

You fucked me, you used me,
Turned me black and blue.
You sent me to the hospital,
Had me fighting for my life,
All because you hated **you**.
You belittled me,
You even had me chained and bound to your bullshit.
When I tried to speak up,
That's when you lost your shit.

YOU FUCKING BITCH ASS NIGGA!
You talked so much smack.
Little did I know,
That was you hiding, all the shit you lacked.
I was independent, but you called me crazy.
I tried to grow, but you called me lazy.
Started my own business, you started to hate me.
The more successful I got,
The more you started to haze me.
And grace me with your punches.
I should've listened to my intuition.
I should've listened to my hunches.

KOLANGYET MANMAN'W,
YOU FUCKING KAKA!
You thought your voodoo shit would work and
Turn me into a baka?!
I wish I had a hot bowl of TChaka,
So, I can throw in your face!
Knock you down a few pegs and slow down your pace.

YOU NARCISSISTIC PIECE OF SHIT!
When you hit me the first time, you said that was it!
But I took you back, to make it work for the kids.
I should've have known better,
In between the love bombings,
You would take little digs.
You turned on the stove,
I thought you was bringing the heat.
I can see clearly now, you were just gaslighting me.
Manipulating me to feel sorry for your ass.
When the **FUCK** did you become the victim!?
How long do you think it's gonna last?!

Deep breath

Pardon me for being crass, but I've had enough.
I'm stepping into my own and I'm calling your buff.

I know, life as a single parent won't be easy,
But I know, it won't treat me this greazy.
Lord, give me the strength I need,
So, I won't ever concede
To a person like that,
Who walked all over me, like I was a freakin' doormat.

Give me the attitude of gratitude,
So, I can manifest my healing.
And show me all the intentions,
That my enemies are concealing.

Allow me to Rise like the Phoenix,
From the ashes through the flames
To stand in my glory and not feel ashamed.
Today, I stand before you as a woman,
Who was scorned,
And now, I stand before you as a woman Reborn.

The Phoenix is an immortal bird associated with Greek mythology that cyclically regenerates or is otherwise born again. Associated with the sun, a Phoenix obtains new life by arising from the ashes of its predecessor.

Translation

Inappropriateness

Ou pa menm fout konem
"You don't even freaking know me."

Se kalite moun sa,
"It's those type of people"

Poukisa ou pa just fèmen bouch ou
"Why don't you just shut your mouth"

Demaskew nan figim
"Get out of my face."

Translation

<u>Her Story</u>

KOLANGYET MANMAN'W,
"Fuck you or fuck you motherfucker or Fuck your
mother!"

KAKA
"Shit"

Baka
"Beast or cow"

TChaka
"Hot soup made of different types of beans"

About the Author

Emma Desulme is a Haitian American woman who's always had the knack of creativity from music, crafting and writing. She is the author of Soul of a Rising Phoenix, a poetry collection that displays an interesting range of emotions, struggles, victories, and experiences that a lot of people go through silently in life.

Emma also discovered a creative new genre in which she incorporated both of her Creole and English languages to bring to you Crenglish Poetry.

When Emma isn't busy writing, you'll find her playing one out of the nine musical instruments, with her community band. Most of her instruments were self- taught.

She makes and wears many hats. You can also find her crocheting while watching anime for her business, Savvy Creations by Emma. If she's not tied up with those other activities, you'll find her teaching people how to save lives using CPR/ First Aid as a certified Instructor for the American Heart Association. Not to mention, she's a bit of a travel junkie.

At a young age, she utilized the tools at her disposal and entered the world of poetry. Growing up, she often felt misunderstood and couldn't quite find the words to express herself. Writing became her escape, her relief and confidant. With her faith in God, Emma began her journey of personal growth, overcoming many challenges and hardships. Her poetry book is a physical representation of her releasing the very things that used to bind and keep her from greatness. She hopes that her readers can be inspired to do the very things that frightens them the most and step out of their comfort zone.

Rather it is to write that book, perform that song or start that business. Emma is a firm believer that, if your dreams aren't intimidating to you, chances are it's insulting God.

Let's Get Social!

Website- www.soulofarisingphoenix.com
Email-info.soulofarisingphoenix@gmail.com

Facebook & Instagram- Soul of a Rising Phoenix

"It is your destiny, your birthright, to step out of your comfort zone and into the spotlight. To no longer feel bewildered and ashamed but to rise from the ashes through the flames, with all your glory and fame. Rise."

-*Emma Desulme*

www.ingramcontent.com/pod-product-compliance
Lightning Source LLC
Chambersburg PA
CBHW060427090426
42734CB00011B/2476